Sheep

Tessa Potter and Donna Bailey

STECK-VAUGHN
LIBRARY
A Division of Steck-Vaughn Company

This farmer has a lot of sheep.
The sheep live together in a flock.

2

In summer the sheep live up in the hills.
They eat grass.

Now it is winter.

It is snowing.

The farmer must bring the sheep
down from the hills.

The farmer has a sheep dog to help him.
The dog finds one of the sheep
lost in the snow.

The dog and the farmer bring the sheep
down to the fields near the farm.

The snow covers the ground.
The sheep can't eat the grass.
The farmer will give them hay to eat.

The sheep have thick, woolly coats
to keep them warm in the snow.

8

Now it is nearly spring.

The lambs will be born soon.

The farmer puts all the mother sheep
together in a field.

The mother sheep are called ewes.
Look at this ewe.
She is going to have some lambs.
The farmer puts her in a lambing pen.

These lambs have just been born.
The ewe has two lambs to take care of.

The ewe licks one of her lambs.
She does not want to take care of
the other lamb.
The farmer takes it away.

This lamb lies by the ewe.
It can drink her milk.

The other lamb is called a bum lamb.
The farmer feeds the bum lamb.
He gives it milk in a bottle.

When the weather is warmer, the ewes and
the lambs go back to the field.
The lambs stay close to their mothers.
They still drink milk from the ewes.

The farmer has put hay in the field.

The lambs like to jump on the hay.

They nestle into the hay to keep warm.

Later they will learn to eat the hay.

Now the lambs are six weeks old.
They do not need to drink milk
from the ewes.
They eat the hay and the new grass.
They grow big and strong.

It is summer, and it is hot.
The sheep do not need
their long, thick coats.
It's time to cut off their wool.
The farmer and his dog round up the sheep.

18

The farmer brings the sheep from
the hills down to the shearing shed.

These sheep are in a pen.
They are waiting to go
into the shearing shed.

20

The first sheep are in
the shearing shed.
The men cut off their wool
with electric scissors.

A sheep's coat is called a fleece.
It takes four minutes
to cut off a fleece.

22

When the men cut off a sheep's fleece,
it does not hurt the sheep.
It will soon grow a new coat.

The fleeces are rolled and
put into bags to be sold.
People in different parts of the world
use wool to make cloth.

24

This woman is combing some wool
to get all the tangles out.

This woman is spinning the wool.
Her spinning wheel twists and
pulls the wool into a thin thread.

This man is weaving wool threads
into cloth.
He is using a hand loom.

Look at all these balls of wool.
They are being used in
a weaving factory to make cloth.
The girl is making sure that
the threads are not broken.

These balls of wool have been dyed.
The weavers use the different colors
to make patterns in the cloth.

People also use wool to make
rugs and carpets.
This woman is making a carpet by hand.

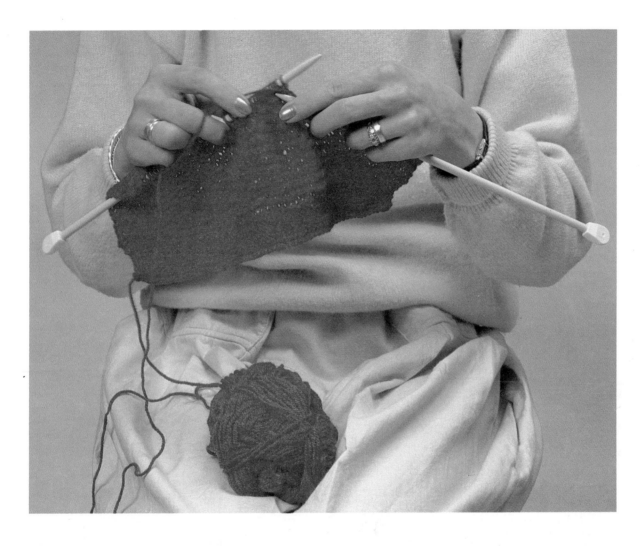

We use wool for knitting, too.
We knit sweaters and hats and
socks with it.

Wool keeps the sheep warm in the winter.

It keeps us warm, too.

Can you see anything in the picture

that is made of wool?

Index

Reading Consultant: Diana Bentley
Editorial Consultant: Donna Bailey
Supervising Editor: Kathleen Fitzgibbon

Illustrated by Gill Tomblin
Picture research by Suzanne Williams
Designed by Richard Garratt Design

Photographs
Cover: Eric and David Hosking
Bruce Coleman: 25 (Gerald Cubitt), 26 (Jennifer Fry), 27 (M. Timothy O'Keefe)
    and 28 (Colin Molyneux)
Farmers Weekly: 22
Frank Lane Picture Agency: 11 (Ray Bird), 18, 19 and 20 (A. J. Roberts),
    21 (Martin B. Withers)
Peter Greenland: 1, 2, 10, 12, 13, 15, 16, 17, 29, 31 and 32
Robert Harding Picture Library: 30
NHPA: 7 and 9 (S. & O. Mathews)
OSF Picture Library: 14 (Raymond Blythe), 23 (Stuart Bebb)
ZEFA: 3, 6 and 8

Library of Congress Cataloging-in-Publication Data: Potter, Tessa. Sheep/Tessa Potter and Donna Bailey; [illustrated by Gill Tomblin]. p. cm.—(Animal world) SUMMARY: Discusses the raising of sheep for wool. ISBN 0-8114-2630-0 1. Sheep—Juvenile literature. 2. Wool—Juvenile literature. [1. Sheep. 2. Wool.] I. Bailey, Donna. II. Tomblin, Gill, ill. III. Title. IV. Series: Animal world (Austin, Tex.) SF375.2.P67 1990 636.3—dc20 89-22022 CIP AC